contents

Before you start

About this book

Have fun creating the projects in this book. Every project is simple to make, using easy-to-find materials. You can design a game to play, jewellery and a crown to wear, decorations for special occasions and models to hold things.

Once you have learned the different ways of making things with straws, enjoy trying out other ideas of your own.

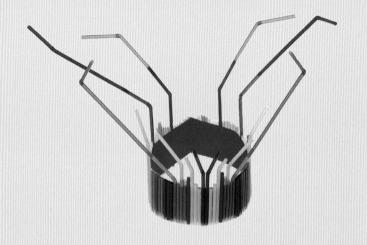

Tools and materials

For these projects you will need coloured plastic straws with bendy ends. Use several packets to make sure you have enough to make everything you want. Useful tools are a pair of scissors, a ruler and some glue. For some projects you will also need coloured modelling clay – use the kind that dries in air.

The tools and materials you will need are listed at the start of each project.

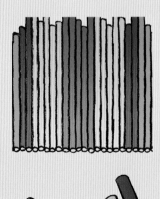

Tips about joining straws

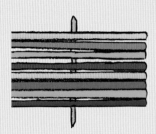 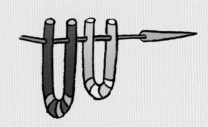 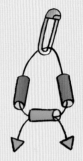

You can push a toothpick through the centre of straws.

You can sew through straws with a needle and thread or thin elastic.

You can thread elastic through straw pieces.

How to fix straws together

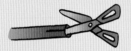

Cut snips in the end of a straw.

Put a drop of glue on the snip.

Push the snipped straw into the end of an unsnipped straw.

Learning logos

The activities in the book provide practice in different skills, identified by the logos below.

An activity practising imagination and creativity

An activity practising fine motor control

An activity practising balancing

An activity involving picturing the body

An activity practising spatial skills

An activity practising pattern making

Funny figures

different coloured straws ● coloured modelling clay
scissors

1 Roll a small bit of modelling clay into a ball.

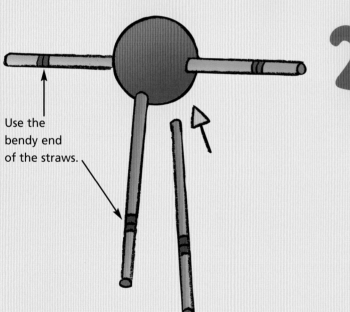

Use the bendy end of the straws.

2 Cut two short pieces of straw for arms and two longer pieces for legs. Push them into the clay ball.

3 Cut two tiny pieces of straw for the eyes and another for the nose. Snip all around the end of another small piece to make hair. Push them all into the clay ball.

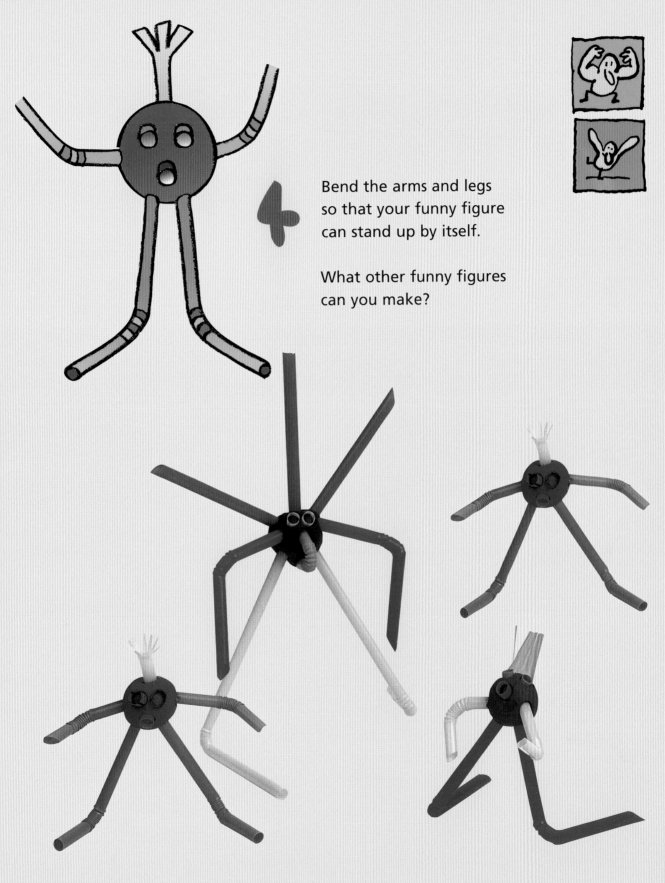

Bend the arms and legs
so that your funny figure
can stand up by itself.

What other funny figures
can you make?

Fancy flowers

different coloured straws ● scissors
wooden skewers ● modelling clay ● ruler

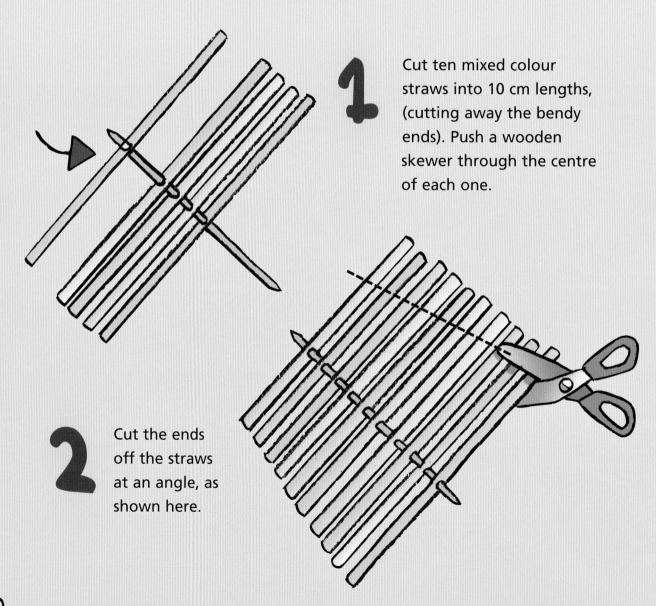

1 Cut ten mixed colour straws into 10 cm lengths, (cutting away the bendy ends). Push a wooden skewer through the centre of each one.

2 Cut the ends off the straws at an angle, as shown here.

3 Twist the straws around the skewer to create flower petals. Push a small ball of modelling clay on to the end of the wooden skewer as the centre of the flower.

4 Roll some clay into a ball. Push a green straw into it. Twist the straw to fill the end with clay. Remove the straw and push the skewer into it.

clown game

round cheese box base ● gouache paint ● paintbrush
different coloured straws ● scissors ● glue
white modelling clay

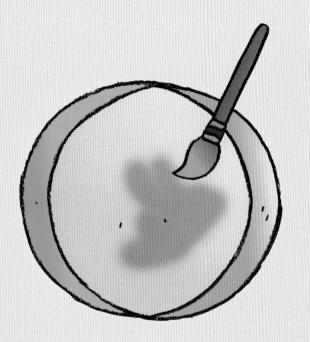

1 Paint the cheese box base on both sides and leave it to dry.

2 Cut off the bendy end of two blue straws to make eyelids. Cut off the end of a red straw for the mouth. Bend and glue them on to the box.

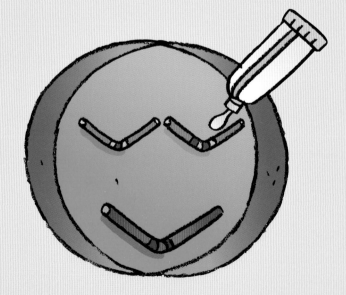

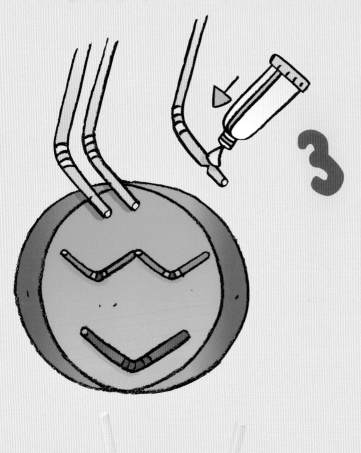

3 Cut some yellow straws in half for hair. Snip a notch near the bendy end and put in a drop of glue. Fit the notch over the rim of the box.

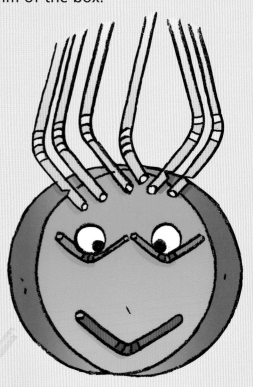

 Roll some white modelling clay into balls for eyes. Paint black dots on them.

HOW TO PLAY THE CLOWN GAME
Put the eyes anywhere in the box. Tilt the box up and down until the eyes fit into their sockets.

straw fish

coloured modelling clay ● different coloured straws scissors

1 Model some clay into an oval shape for the fish's body.

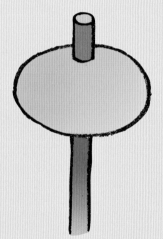

2 Push a straw through the centre of the body to make a hole in it. Remove the straw.

3 Cut short pieces of straw for the eyes and mouth. Push them into place on the body.

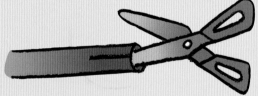

Cut another piece of straw for the tail. Make little snips at one end. Push the other end into the body.

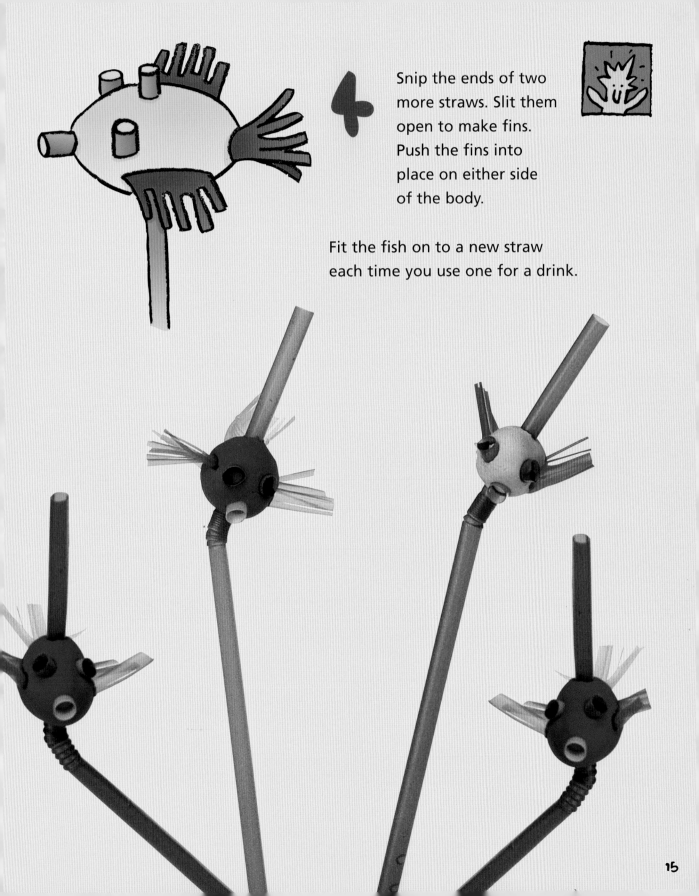

4 Snip the ends of two more straws. Slit them open to make fins. Push the fins into place on either side of the body.

Fit the fish on to a new straw each time you use one for a drink.

Shining stars

12 straws of the same colour for each star
scissors ● glue ● ruler

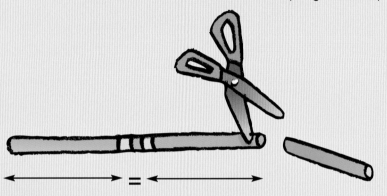

1 Measure the length of the bendy end of a straw, up to the bend. Measure the same length *after* the bend. Cut off the rest of the straw. Cut 12 straws all the same length.

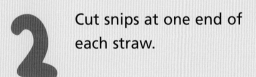

2 Cut snips at one end of each straw.

3 Put a drop of glue on to each of the snipped ends. Join the straws together. Fit the snipped end of one straw into the unsnipped end of another.

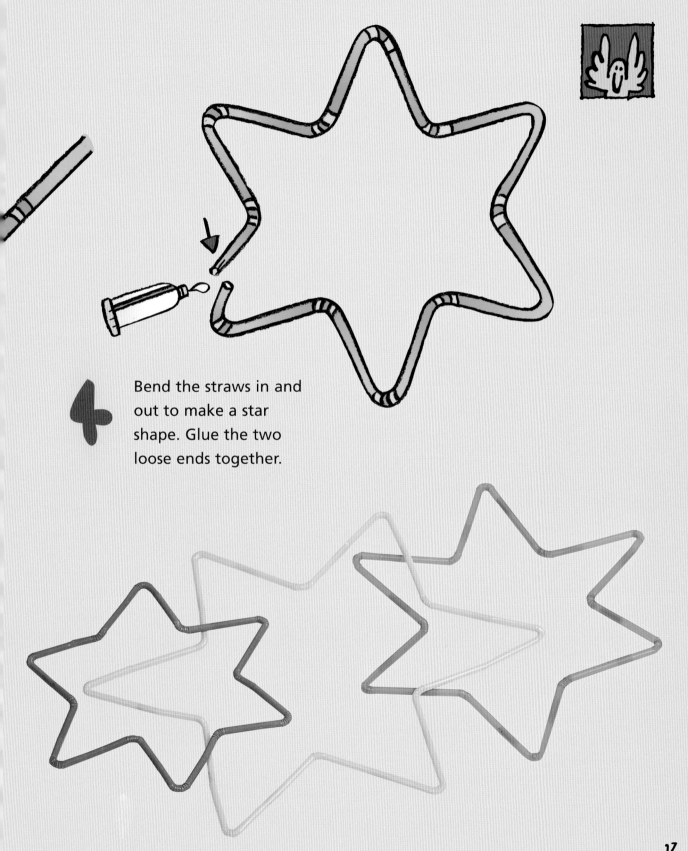

Bend the straws in and out to make a star shape. Glue the two loose ends together.

crooked crown

coloured card ● scissors ● glue ● different coloured straws

1 Cut a piece of card – as wide as your hand and just longer than the size of your head.

Cut a slit at both ends – halfway *down* from the top edge of the card and halfway *up* from the bottom edge.

2 Cut straws into different lengths (the smallest must be long enough to hide the card).

Spread glue on the card and arrange the straws side by side, up to the slits.

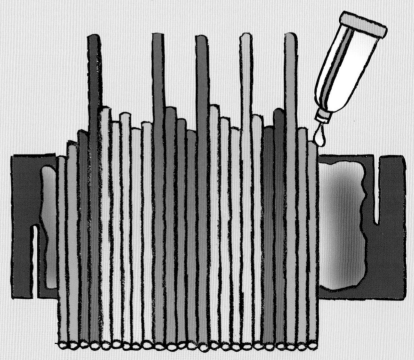

18

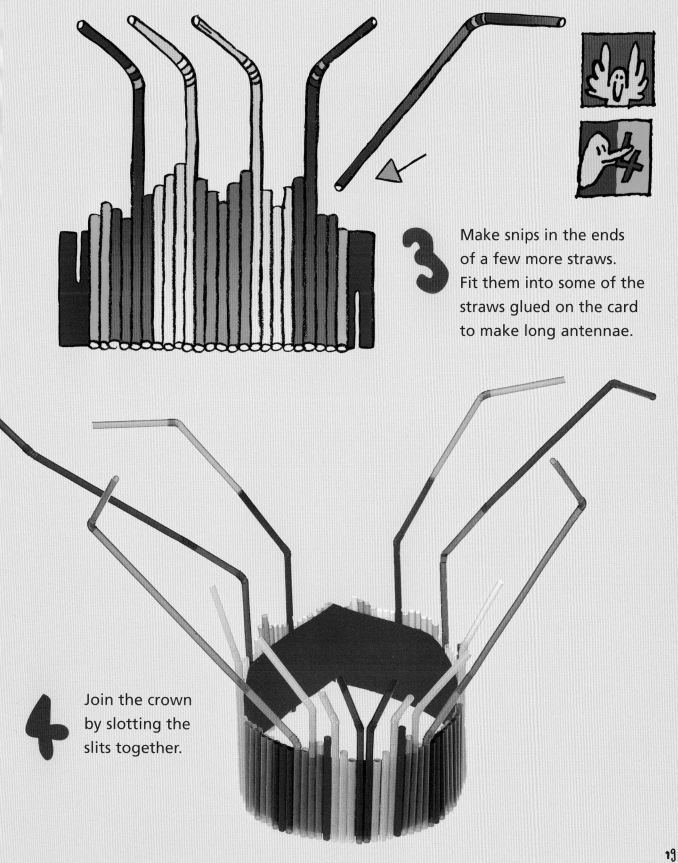

3 Make snips in the ends of a few more straws. Fit them into some of the straws glued on the card to make long antennae.

4 Join the crown by slotting the slits together.

19

Fabulous frame

blue, yellow green and red straws
ruler ● scissors ● glue

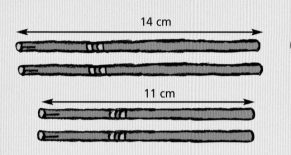

14 cm

11 cm

1 Make snips in the bendy end of four blue straws. Measure the straws and cut off the unsnipped ends to make two straws 14 cm long and the other two 11 cm long.

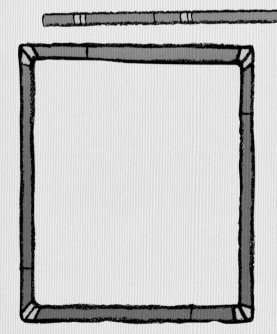

2 Fit the straws into one another – one long, then one short. Bend them into a rectangle.

3 Make a yellow rectangle in the same way. Push the straws further into one another, so that this rectangle fits inside the blue one. Make a green rectangle that fits inside the yellow one.

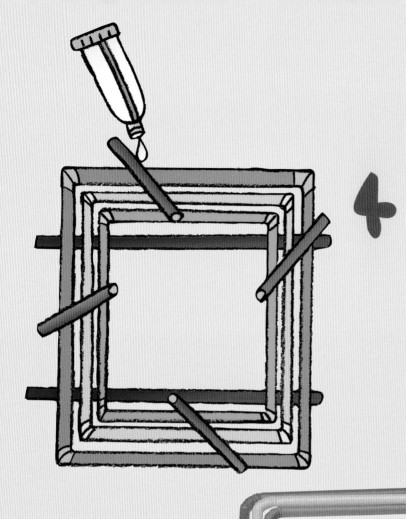

4 Glue two long red straws on to the back of the frame to hold the three rectangles together.

Turn the frame over and glue a short piece of red straw diagonally across each side.

Glue one of your photos or pictures on to the centre of the frame.

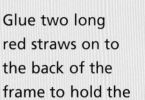

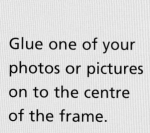

Bendy bracelet

scissors ● red, blue, yellow and green straws
1 m thin elastic ● safety pin ● ruler

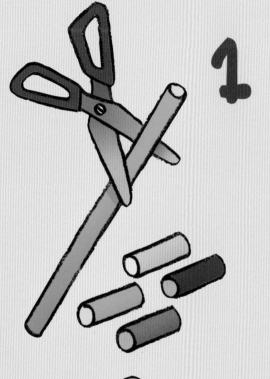

1 Cut each straw into 1 cm pieces. Bend the elastic in two and pin it to something fixed, for example a safety pin. Thread a piece of straw (each of the same colour) on to each end of the elastic. Cross the ends of the elastic and thread them through a green piece.

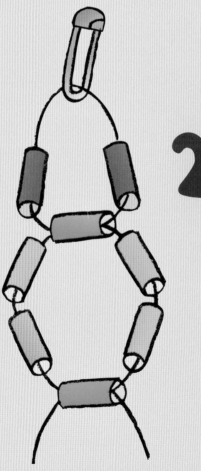

2 Change colour again and thread two pieces over each end of the elastic. Cross the ends again through a green piece.

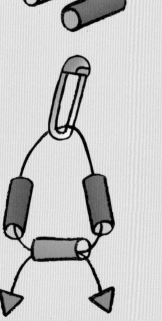

22

3 Keep threading pieces in the same way, using each colour in turn, until the bracelet is long enough to fit around your wrist.

4 After crossing the ends of the elastic through the last green piece, cross them again through a 2 cm long red piece (cut from another straw). Knot the ends of the elastic.

Join the bracelet by slotting the two pieces at the other end through the long piece.

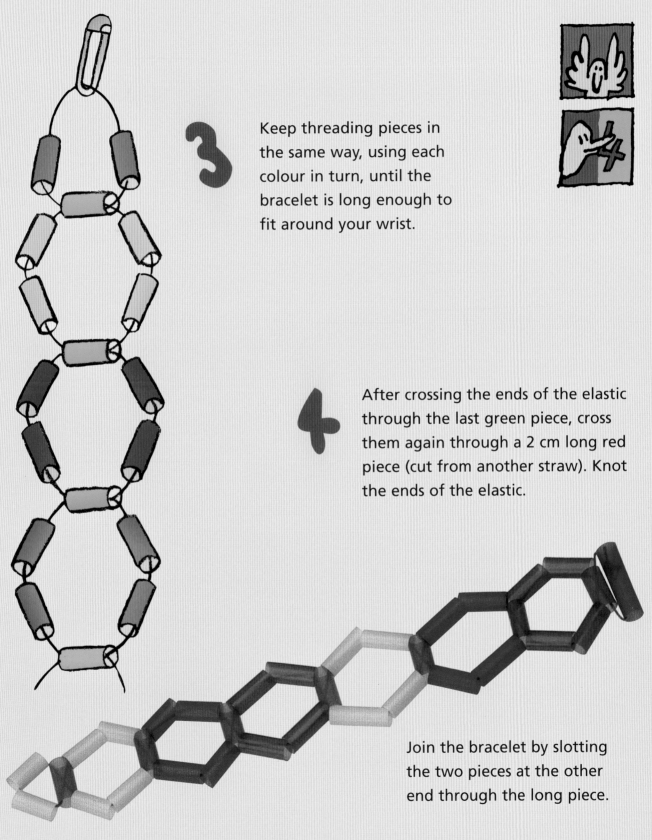

Nifty necklace

red, blue, green and yellow straws ● scissors
thin, round elastic ● thick needle ● ruler

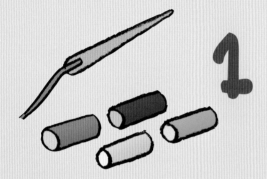

1 Cut blue, red, yellow and green straws into 2 cm pieces. Thread a thick needle with a 60 cm length of thin elastic.

2 Bend and cut: **two green straws** about 2 cm away from the bendy bit; **two red straws** about 3 cm away from the bendy bit; **two blue straws** about 4 cm from the bendy bit; **one yellow straw** about 4.5 cm from the bendy bit.

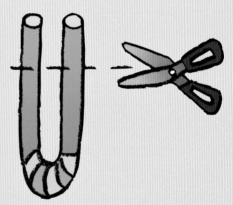

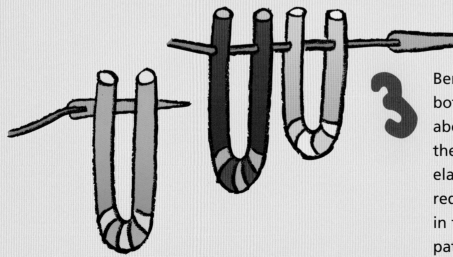

3 Bend all the straws. Pierce both ends of the green straw about half a centimetre from the tip. Pull through half the elastic. Do the same with the red, yellow and blue straws in turn to make the necklace pattern.

24

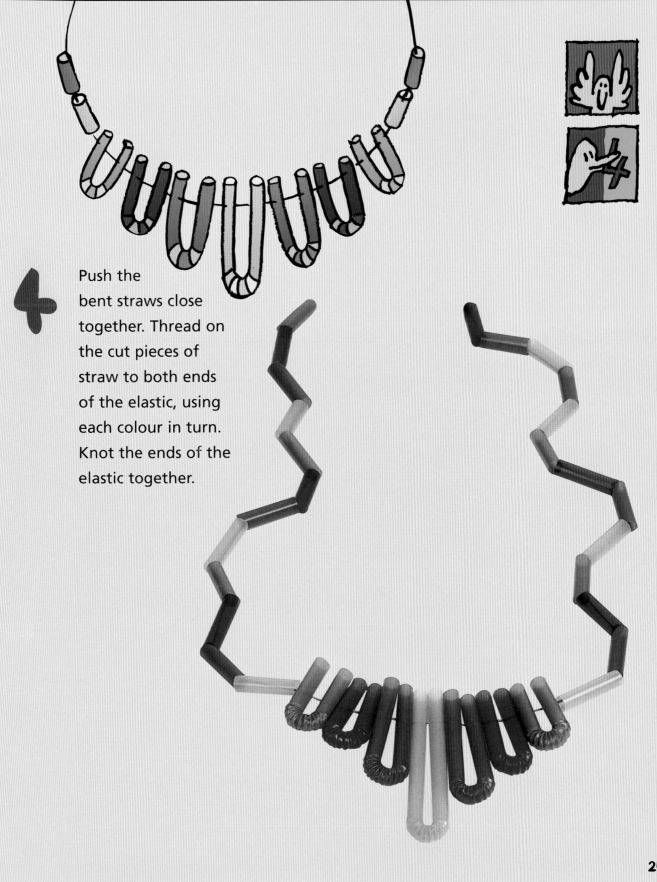

4 Push the bent straws close together. Thread on the cut pieces of straw to both ends of the elastic, using each colour in turn. Knot the ends of the elastic together.

Racing raft

yellow, green and blue straws ● scissors ● thick white glue
modelling clay ● white plastic cup ● ruler

1 Cut about 16 yellow straws 15 cm long and two green straws 12 cm long. Roll out some clay into a slab. Push both ends of each straw firmly into the slab. Twist the straws to fill the ends with a blobs of clay.

2 Lay the yellow straws side by side, making a rectangle. Keep them in place with two rolls of modelling clay and coat the straws with glue. Glue the green straws across the mast, as shown. Leave the raft to dry.

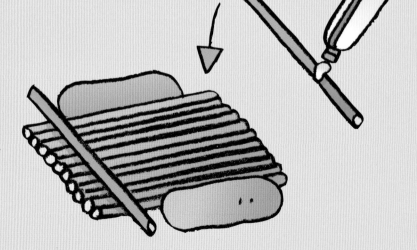

26

3 Cut a sail from a white plastic cup. Slit a blue straw along half its length for the mast. Slot the sail into the mast.

4 Cut a small piece of yellow straw and put it on top of the mast. Cut a blue straw a few centimetres from its bendy bit and glue it along the middle of the raft – but only as far as the bendy bit. Bend the straw upwards and fit the mast into its end.

The raft is ready to sail!

whirling windmill

different coloured straws ● scissors
2 toothpicks or wooden skewers ● ruler

1 **The base**
Bend and cut a blue straw 3 cm from either side of the bendy bit.

Snip the long end of two other straws. Fit the ends into the bent straw.

Bend the other end of the two straws. Make slits at the end of one of them and push it into the end of the other one.

2 **The wings**
Find 8 straws of alternate colours. Cut them up to the bendy bit. Push a skewer through the centre of them. Cut 1 cm off the ends on both sides.

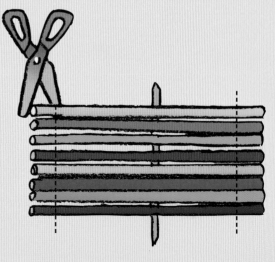

28

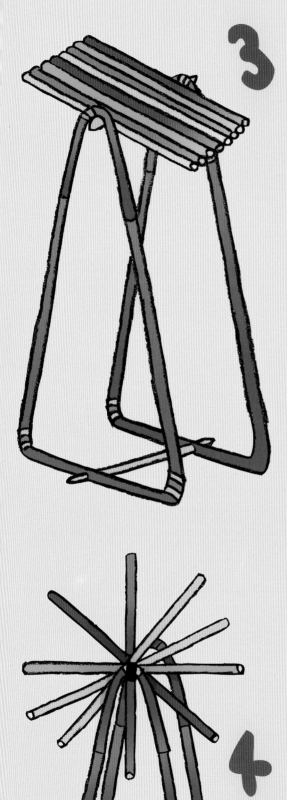

3 Join the two triangles at their base with a toothpick. Push the toothpick at the ends of the wings into the top point of the two triangles.

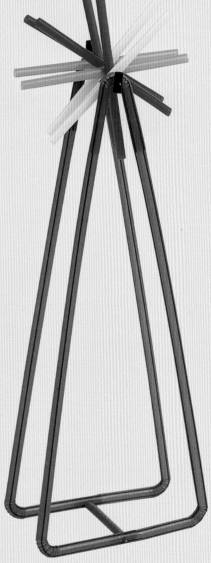

4 Spread out the wings one colour at a time. Cut two small pieces of straw and fit one on each end of the toothpick. Now your windmill is ready to turn!

index

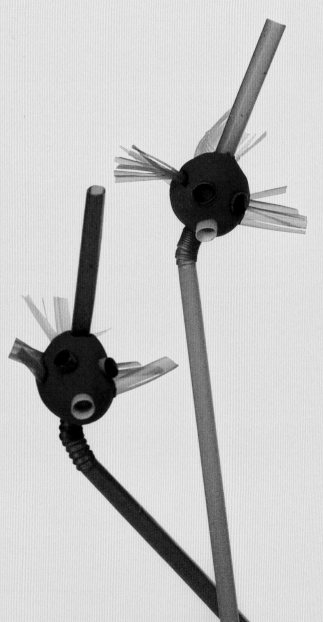

30